Pop's Gloss

By Sally Cowan

T0342846

Ash and Dad rushed to pick up Pop at Doc Glen's.

"Pop!" said Ash. "I am glad to see you!"

But Pop looked glum.

"I fell down at the shop
and hit my leg," Pop said.

"You can go home,"
said Doc Glen.
"But put your leg up!"

"I rub gloss on my van,"
said Pop.
"I got the pot at the shop.
But then I fell down."

When Pop got home,
he had a long nap.

"Let's rub the gloss
on Pop's van!" said Ash.

Ash and Dad got big globs of gloss.

Rub, rub, rub!

Pop was glad.

CHECKING FOR MEANING

1. Why was Pop at Doc Glen's? *(Literal)*

2. What did Ash suggest doing while Pop was having a nap? *(Literal)*

3. How did Pop feel when he saw his glossy van? How do you know? *(Inferential)*

EXTENDING VOCABULARY

gloss	What does *gloss* mean? What is another word with a similar meaning? E.g. shine.
glad	What is a word from the story that begins with *gl–* and has the opposite meaning to *glad*?
glam	Explain that *glam* is the short form of the word *glamorous*. What other words do we sometimes shorten? E.g. fab for fabulous.

MOVING BEYOND THE TEXT

1. Why did Doc Glen tell Pop to *put your leg up*? How would this help Pop's leg?

2. Have you ever had an injury that stopped you doing something you really wanted to do? What happened?

3. What words can you think of to describe Ash? E.g. kind, thoughtful, helpful.

4. How do you think Ash felt when she did a job for Pop without being asked? Have you ever done that for someone? How did you feel?

SPEED SOUNDS

bl	gl	cr	fr	st

PRACTICE WORDS

glad

Glen's

glum

globs

gloss

glam

Glen